Beading is a double-pleasure: you have the joy of creating something lovely, and then you get to re-experience that joy every time you wear the jewelry you've created, or see your friends wearing it. Creating is like air to me. I feel so much better after spending some time doing something creative; it improves my outlook and everything else in my life goes more smoothly. I slipped in a few drawings and photos just for fun. Hope you like them! And I hope you enjoy taking inspiration from the pages in this book. I'd love to see your creations. Upload pictures to my facebook page, *Awesome Beading Patterns.* Meet other people who love to bead just like you! I look forward to seeing your creations!

--Lisa

BASIC STITCHES

RIGHT ANGLE WEAVE

Step 1.

Pick up 8 beads. Leaving a 4 inch or so tail, tie a knot so that the 8 beads form a circle. (Eventually this circle will become a square.) Work the needle through 4 beads so that the knot and tail is at the bottom, and the needle is coming out at the top.

Step 2.

Pick up 6 beads. Work needle through the top two beads of the previous step, then up two beads on the side, and across two beads at the new top. The thread should be coming out at the top, as in the previous step, but it should be coming out on the opposite side. Repeat step 2 until desired length is reached.

CURVED RIGHT ANGLE WEAVE

Curved Right Angle Weave is a variant of Right Angle Weave. Instead of a series of squares, you create a series of trapezoids, which together create curved lines instead of straight lines. This is achieved by having one side with an extra bead, so that side is longer than its opposing side.

Step 1.

Pick up 9 beads. Leaving a 4 inch or so tail, tie a knot so that the 9 beads form a circle. Work the needle through so that the knot and tail are at the bottom, and the thread comes through at the top. You should have 2 beads at the bottom and top, 2 beads on 1 side and 3 beads on the other side. The side with 3 beads will form the outer part of the curve.

Step 2.

Pick up 7 beads. Work needle up through the top two beads of the previous step. Then work needle through so that it is coming out the top. It should come out the opposite side from the previous step. Repeat step 2 until desired length is achieved. If forming a circle, the 3 beads will always be on the same side. If forming an S or serpentine shape, the 3 beads will sometimes be on one side and sometimes another. Just remember that the 3 beads always form the outside of the curve.

LAYING ON CRYSTALS OR ACCENT BEADS

Many of the designs in this book have a foundation made with Right Angle Weave, and then a layer on top of crystals or other interesting accent beads. This accent bead occupies the center of each square (or trapezoid in the case of Curved Right Angle Weave),

Step 1.

With thread coming out of the corner of one of your squares

(or trapezoids), pick up 1 size 15 seed bead, 1 4mm accent bead, and 1 size 15 seed bead. Go to opposite corner and weave thread through two beads at the bottom, and then up through two beads on the side (or three if it is the outer side of curved right angle weave), coming out at the corner where the first size 15 seed bead is. Alternatively, you can weave the thread up the left side and over the top. Just make sure that the accent bead is in the center of your square or trapezoid, with the thread going through diagonally.

Step 2.

For greater strength and security, weave the thread diagonally a second time through the size 15 seed bead, 4mm accent bead, and size 15 seed bead. Weave thread through two beads shared with the adjacent square or trapezoid, ready to start the next square or trapezoid.

Repeat steps 1 and two until all desired squares or trapezoids are done.

SMOOTHING EDGES

Neaten up the edges of your piece by weaving a size 15 seed bead in the gaps between the squares or trapezoids. If doing Curved Right Angle Weave, skip this step on the inside curve.

STRAIGHT STITCH

Step 1.

Pick up first row. Pick up first bead of second row. Work thread through last bead of first row, and again through the first bead of the second row.

Step 2.

 Pick up second bead of second row. Work thread through second-to-last bead of first row, and back through second bead of second row.

Repeat until row two is complete.

Step 3.

 When the end of the second row is reached, weave thread back through the entire first row, then thread it through the entire second row. This will strengthen the weave.

STRENGTHENING

Every so often as you weave, tie a knot in your thread. When the piece is completely put together, weave any straggling loose threads back through for additional strength.

TIP

Never force the needle through if it is tight. You may break a bead. Try finding an alternate path for your thread. If this is not an option, you need a thinner needle, thinner thread, or beads with larger holes.

Criss

Cross

Bracelet

CRISS-CROSS BRACELET

This very simple and elegant design works well with casual and dressy attire. Celebrate your favorite team and make the bracelet in the team's colors! The bracelet works well with two different tones of the same basic color, or with two very different colors. You will have a lot of fun picking out the seed beads and crystals, and then seeing it all come together.

SUPPLIES AND TOOLS

These quantities are for a 7-inch bracelet. You can easily make this bracelet shorter or longer by adjusting quantities accordingly. You need a very thin needle and very thin Fireline, as you will be going through some of the beads several times. Unless you are using dark crystals, use the Crystal color Fireline. Otherwise you will see dark lines showing through the crystals.

40 4mm bicone crystals in color A

39 4mm bicone crystals in color B

Size 11 seed beads in color A

Size 11 seed beads in color B

Size 15 seed beads in color A

Size 15 seed beads in color B

Clasp (I tend to use slider clasps with 4 loops on each side)

Size 12 needle

Fireline 6LB/SIZE D .008" avg.dia. Crystal

NOTES

These illustrations show space between the beads. This is to help you see the path of the thread. When you create your piece you will want the beads rather snug. Gray beads and black thread indicate steps you've already completed.

Step 1.

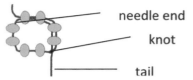

needle end

knot

tail

Pick up 8 size 11 seed beads in color A. Leaving a 4 to 6 inch tail, tie a knot, forming a circle with the beads. Place the knot at the bottom of your piece, then thread the needle through 4 of the beads, and come out at the corner opposite the knot, at the top. These last two beads form the first "ladder rung" of the right-angle weave.

Step 2.

Pick up 2 size 11 seed beads in color A, 2 in color B, and 2 in color A. Thread the needle through the top 2 beads from step 1, and through the first 4 beads you just picked up. The thread should now be coming out the top, on the opposite side that it came out in step 1.

Step 3.

Pick up 6 size 11 seed beads in color B. Thread the needle through the top 2 beads from step 2, and through the first 4 beads you just picked up. The thread should come out the top, on the same side as step 1, the opposite side of step 2.

Step 4.

Pick up 6 size 11 seed beads in color A. Thread the needle through the top 2 beads from the previous step, and through the first 4 beads you just picked up. The thread should come out the top, on the opposite side as the previous step.

Step 5.

Pick up 6 size 11 seed beads in color A. Thread the needle through the top 2 beads from the previous step, and through the first 2 beads you just picked up. The thread should come out through the top of one of the sides, on the same side as in the previous step. You have completed your first leg! You should have 4 squares done in color A, and one in color B. The color B square should be in the center. Don't worry too much if they don't look exactly like squares yet. Your next leg will be done entirely in color A.

Step 6.

Pick up 6 beads in color A. Thread the needle through the first 2 beads picked up in the previous step, and through the first 4 you just picked up. Sharing the first square with the first leg, you now have 2 squares done on your second leg.

Step 7.

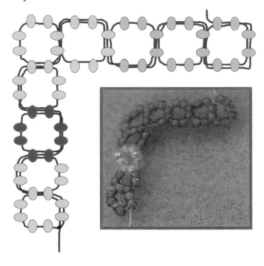

Finish up the second leg according to the diagram, all in color A. After the last square, your thread should be poised to start a new leg perpendicular to the leg you just finished, and parallel to the first leg.

Mind the Gap!

Until you reach the finishing step, be sure your thread does not cross this gap between two squares.

Step 8.

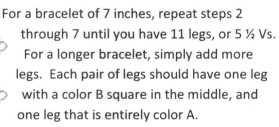

For a bracelet of 7 inches, repeat steps 2 through 7 until you have 11 legs, or 5 ½ Vs. For a longer bracelet, simply add more legs. Each pair of legs should have one leg with a color B square in the middle, and one leg that is entirely color A.

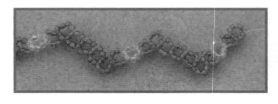

Step 9.

You are done with size 11 beads in color A! Work the thread back through the last three squares you did, so that thread comes out from the side of the middle square. This may be a color A square or a color B square, depending on whether you made an odd or an even number of legs in steps 1 through 8. Now the thread is poised to add the first square in a set of legs that will cross the set you made in the previous steps.

This bracelet works well with very similar colors such as the khaki/olivine shown at far left, two contrasting tones of the same color, or two completely different colors.

Step 10.

Pick up 6 size 11 beads in color B. Work thread back through the side beads of the square of the last leg 2 middle from step 8. Work through the first 4 beads just picked up. Pick up 6 more size 11 beads in color B. Work the thread through all 6 beads and back through 4 beads of the previous square. Work thread through the square the intersects both legs, coming out the side of that intersecting square.

Step 11.

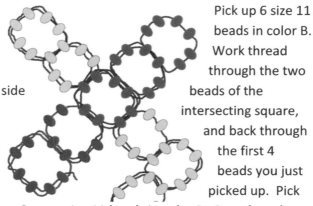

side

Pick up 6 size 11 beads in color B. Work thread through the two beads of the intersecting square, and back through the first 4 beads you just picked up. Pick up 6 more size 11 beads in color B. Pass thread through the 2 beads shared with the previous square, and through all 6 beads just picked up. Your thread should come out pointing toward the leg it is about to intersect.

Step 12.

side

Pick up 2 size 11 beads in color B. Work thread through the two beads of the intersecting square. Pick up 2 more size 11 beads in color B. Work thread through the last 2 beads you picked up in step 11, and the first 2 beads you just picked up.

If it feels too tight to get your needle through, don't force it. Better to have a bit of thread showing on the underside than to break beads.

Step 13.

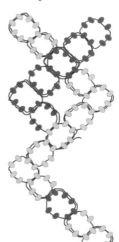

Work thread through 6 of the beads on the intersecting square, so that the thread comes out the other side.

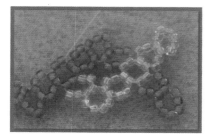

Step 14.

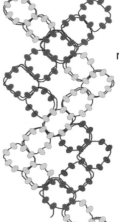

Repeat steps 10 through 13, working in color B, until the length of the bracelet has been reached. Add 2 more squares after the last intersection.

Step 15.

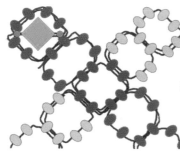

Now you are done with size 11 seed beads! Pick up 1 size 15 seed bead in the color matching the size 11 seed beads of the square where your thread is. Pick up 1 4mm bicone crystal in the same color, and another size 15 seed bead. Entering at the opposite corner, work the thread

through 4 size 11 beads of the square. Go through the 15, crystal, and 15 again, for reinforcement. Work the thread through the two beads that the

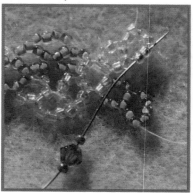

current square shares with the adjacent square. Lay on all crystals in this manner, using color A size 15

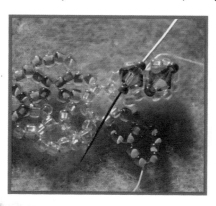

beads and color A crystals to lay on the color A size 11 beads, and color B 15s and crystals to lay on the color B 11s. In this example, khaki crystals are going

on the light beads, and olivine will go on the darker beads.

Step 16.

Now you may cross the gap! To create a clean edge, weave the thread through all the edges, picking up size 15 seed beads to fill in the gaps between all the squares. Use color A 15s to fill the gaps between color A squares, and color B 15s to fill the gaps between color B squares. It is sometimes easier to do this step from the back of the piece.

Step 17.

Attach your clasp! Slider clasps with 4 loops work well for this bracelet. String on several size 15 seed beads and work your thread through the loops a few times.

Step 18.

Weave any loose ends through the piece, tying knots as needed. Clip all loose ends of thread.

Most Important Step

Enjoy!

Variations

on a theme

SERPENTINE

Two simple modifications to the basic criss-cross bracelet design result in a softer, more serpentine look.

Modification 1.

On the corners, instead of making a 4-sided square, you make a 3-sided shape. Two edges have 2 beads, the third (outside) edge has 3 beads which form a curve.

Modification 2.

Orient the crystals lengthwise. The size 15 seed beads that go on either side of the crystal should be oriented towards the clasp.

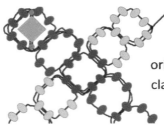

Optional Modification.

Use round beads instead of bicones. This will soften up the curves even more.

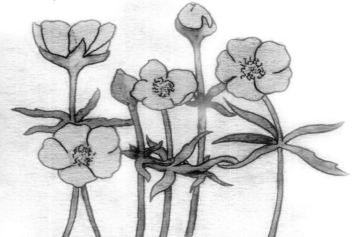

EARRINGS

Shorten the length to 2 Vs and attach to earring findings. The earrings pictured here were made with Erinite AB and Light Azore AB crystals. The Erinite crystals were oriented horizontally, and the Azore were oriented vertically, for an interesting texture change.

WATCH

Watch faces can be found in most places beads are sold. Simply attach the beaded segments to the watch similarly as you would to a clasp, using the same thread you used to weave the beads . Each beaded section of the watch pictured here measures 4 ½ Vs. The finished piece is 7 inches long. This watch is made with glass pearls in addition to crystals. Any 4mm bead will work.

CHOKER

Vampire Bite Choker

To make the vampire bite choker pictured, use Jet AB and Black Diamond crystals. Positioned a bit off center are two Siam-colored crystals representing the vampire bites.

Dripping down from the bite marks are red size 11 seed beads, ending in Siam drop crystals.

Length

The length for a choker will be approximately twice as long as a bracelet. The choker pictured here is 12 Vs, or 24 diamonds long; the beaded portion is 13 ¼ inches.

Clasp

The addition of chain and use of a hook or lobster

clasp makes it easy to adjust the length of the choker when you put it on. It will be easier to use this type of clasp if the beaded portion of the piece ends in a point, rather than two open legs as with the bracelet. Attach jump rings to each end. To one jump ring, attach the lobster or hook clasp. To the other jump ring, attach a length of chain about 2 inches long. If desired, wire wrap some beads to dangle off the end of the chain.

LATTICE BUNHOLDER

The lattice bunholder is worked with a right-angle weave foundation and layered crystals like the bracelet, in a lattice pattern. It is attached to an elastic pony-tail holder. Four jump rings are woven in for attaching optional dangling focal beads.

Foundation

Edges

The edges are finished with the size 15 seed beads just as for the bracelet, except for the 4 top corners of the middle "windows" in the lattice work. Instead of a size 15 seed bead, weave in a closed jump ring. These will be used to dangle charms or focal beads.

The foundation is worked in right angle weave, with lines intersecting at every 5th square. The longest lines (intersecting in the middle of the piece) are 31 squares long. The next longest lines are 27 squares long, and the shortest are 17 squares long. The piece pictured has the foundation done in one color, as the inspiration for the piece was white lattice, however it could be done in two colors.

Attach to Ponytail Holder

Attach each loose end of the lattice piece to the ponytail holder using straight stitched size 11 seed beads. Use 4 beads in each row. For the piece pictured, 8 rows were required to attach each end.

Crystals

The crystals are laid on exactly as they are in the bracelet. For the piece pictured, clear AB crystals were placed in a vertical orientation on lines going from upper-left to lower right, and opal AB crystals were placed in a horizontal orientation on the lines going from upper-right to lower-left.

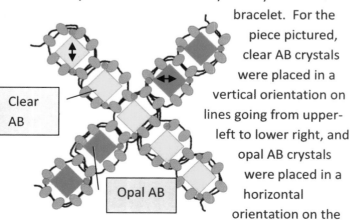

Clear AB

Opal AB

Dangle Charms

Wire wrap focal beads to very small lobster claw clasps. When desired, attach the charms to the 4 jump rings woven into the piece. Or wear without the charms for a simpler look.

Purple

Lupine

Barrette

PURPLE LUPINE BARRETTE

Of course you can make this barrette in any colors you like! I just named it "Purple Lupine Barrette" because it was inspired by a beautiful picture of many shades of purple lupines surrounded by lush greenery. You will use many of the same techniques as other projects in this book. You will also add some new twists - the graduated colors and the scalloped fringe.

SUPPLIES AND TOOLS

62 4mm bicone crystals:

- 12 in a dark shade of color A
- 12 in a medium shade of color A
- 10 in a light shade of color A
- 13 in clear
- 5 in a dark shade of color B
- 5 in a medium shade of color B
- 5 in a light shade of color B

Size 11 seed beads in 4 shades of color A, and 4 shades of color B

Size 15 seed beads. In the pictured piece, I used one shade of green, and 4 shades of purple.

Barrette finding

Size 12 needle

Fireline 6LB/SIZE D .008" avg.dia. Crystal

E6000 or other strong glue

Step 1.

Pick up 8 size 11 seed beads in the darkest shade of color A. Leaving a 4 to 6 inch tail, tie a knot, forming a circle with the beads. Place the knot at the bottom of your piece, then thread the needle through 4 of the beads, and come out at the corner opposite the knot, at the top.

Step 2.

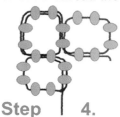

Pick up 6 size 11 seed beads in the darkest shade of color A. Thread the needle through the top 2 beads from step 1, and all 6 beads just picked up.

Step 3.

Pick up 6 size 11 seed beads in the darkest shade of color A. Thread the needle through the last 2 beads from step 2, and the first 2 beads just picked up.

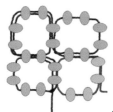

Step 4.

Pick up 4 size 11 seed beads in the darkest shade of color A. Thread the needle through the nearest 2 beads from step 1, the nearest 2 beads from step 3, and the first 2 beads just added.

Step 5.

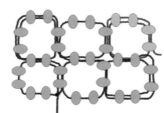

Pick up 6 size 11 seed beads in the medium-dark shade of color A. Thread the needle through the nearest 2 beads from step 4, through all 6 beads just picked up, and through the 2 nearest beads from step 3.

Step 6.

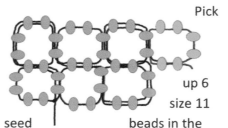

Pick up 4 size 11 seed beads in the medium-dark shade of color A. Thread the needle through the nearest 2 beads from step 5, the nearest 2 beads from step 3, and all 4 beads just picked up.

Step 7.

Pick up 6 size 11 seed beads in the medium-dark shade of color A. Thread the needle through the nearest 2 beads from step 6, and through the first 2 beads you just picked up.

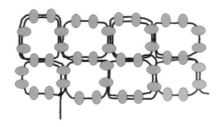

Step 8.

Pick up 4 size 11 seed beads in the medium-dark shade of color A. Thread the needle through the nearest 2 beads from step 5, the nearest 2 beads from step 7, and the first 2 beads just picked up.

Step 9.

Repeat steps 5 through 8 in the following color sequence:

- Medium-light color A
- Light color A
- Dark color B
- Medium-dark color B
- Medium-light color B
- Light color B
- Dark color A
- Medium-dark color A
- Medium-light color A
- Light color A

Step 10.

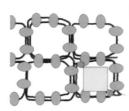

Pick up a size 15 seed bead, a 4mm clear bicone crystal, and another size 15 seed bead. Orient these beads diagonally, and thread the needle through 2 sides of the square. Thread it again through the 15, crystal and other 15. Thread it through 1 side of the square, with the thread coming out between the 2 end squares, ready to layer on to the next square.

Step 11.

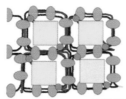

Layer the 3 adjacent squares with size 15 seed beads and clear crystals, oriented in the same direction as the first one. The thread should come out poised to layer on to the next darker shade of color A.

Step 12.

The next 4 squares are layered with the crystals oriented perpendicularly to the set of 4 just

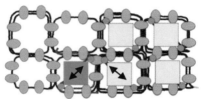

finished. Thread the needle through the 2 outer edge beads of the next square before picking up the size 15 bead, crystal and size 15 bead. Use the light shade of color A crystals.

Use color A seed beads in whatever shade you have. It isn't

necessary to have 4 shades of the size 15 beads.

Step 13.

Lay on the rest of the crystals and size 15 beads, using the colors and shades of the size 11 beads as a guide to selecting the colors and shades of crystals and size 15 beads. Change the orientation of the crystals each time you change color. There isn't one set thread path for this step, just two basic rules:

1. Go through each crystal twice.
2. Don't cross the gaps.

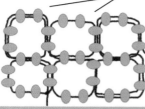

Step 14.

Make the short side edges and the long top edge crisper by weaving size 15 seed beads into the gaps between squares.

Step 15.

Now the fun part! Your bottom edge should still have gaps between the squares. Your scalloped fringe will attach to the main piece in these gaps. Starting at an outside bottom corner of your piece, pick up 13 size 11 seed beads in the darkest shade of color A, 1 crystal in the darkest shade of color A, and 13 more dark color A size 11 beads. Attach the fringe to the main piece at the gap 8 seed beads, 4 squares, or 2 shades in from the edge. Thread needle through 2 of the edge beads, in the direction

from the center of the piece toward the outside of the piece.

Step 16.

Pick up 6 size 11 seed beads in the medium-dark shade of color A, a crystal in the medium-dark shade of color A, and 6 more seed beads. Attach to

the main piece at the gap 2 beads in from the edge, the gap in the middle of the outside-most shade. Thread the needle through 2 of the edge seed beads, in the direction from the outside to the center of the piece. Pick up a size 15 seed bead to fill in the gap. Then thread the needle through the next 2 edge seed beads. The thread should come out where the medium-dark scallop is attached to the main piece.

Step 17.

Pick up 20 size 11 seed beads in the darkest shade of color A, a crystal in the darkest shade of color A, and 20 more seed beads. Attach to the gap in the

middle of the first square of color B. Thread needle through 2 edge beads in the direction from the center to the outside.

Step 18.

Continue in this fashion until all the scallops are complete. Use the guide below, and the photo to determine the colors, shades, number of seed beads, and attach points.

Outer-most scallops (color A, 2 strands)

- *6 beads, 1 crystal, 6 beads, medium-dark*

- *13 beads, 1 crystal, 13 beads, dark*

Next-to-outside scallops (color A, 3 strands)

- *6 beads, 1 crystal, 6 beads, medium-light*

- *12 beads, 1 crystal, 12 beads, medium-dark*

- *20 beads, 1 crystal, 20 beads, dark*

Center scallops (color B, 4 strands)

- *6 beads, 1 crystal, 6 beads, light*

- *14 beads, 1 crystal, 14 beads, medium-light*

- *19 beads, 1 crystal, 19 beads, medium-dark*

- *25 beads, 1 crystal, 25 beads, dark*

There is no one correct path for the needle on this step. Attach to the main piece in the gaps between squares, tie knots to secure, and reinforce by threading through the strands multiple times.

Step 19.

Attach the beaded piece to the barrette finding using glue. Allow to dry. Reinforce by weaving the thread through the edges of the beads and back of the finding.

A 4-inch barrette finding is a good size to use.

Use a glue that makes a strong, permanent bond, that works well with glass and metal.

Braided Barrette

BRAIDED BARRETTE

This simple and unique design can easily be made into a bracelet or choker. Straight stitch three strands in different colors and braid them together to create this textured look. The piece pictured here is done in size 15 seed beads in taupe, yellow, and gold, but any size beads can be used depending on the look you are going for.

SUPPLIES AND TOOLS

Seed beads in three colors (size 15 for the piece pictured)

Size 12 needle

Fireline 6LB/SIZE D .008" avg.dia. Crystal

Barrette finding

E6000 or other strong glue

Step 1.

Pick up one bead and wrap the thread through it to make a stop bead. You will remove this bead later.

Step 2.

Pick up 9 beads in random color order. Pick up 1 bead and start to straight stitch the second row.

Step 3.

Finish the second row with 8 more beads in random color order.

Optional.

If working with very small beads and the thread is tight, skip this step. It may cause you to break a bead. Otherwise, run the needle through the entire first row, and back through the second row. This adds stability to the weave.

Step 4.

You can remove the stop bead now.

Step 5.

Repeat steps 2 through 3 and the optional step if you can, until you have 5 straight stitched rows of 9 beads each in a random pattern of your 3 colors.

Step 6.

Straight stitch 3 beads in color A. This starts one of the legs that will be braided. Stitch this one leg until  you have the length you need. Remember that when it is braided, it will become a little shorter. Stitch the second leg in color B, and the third in color C.

Step 7.

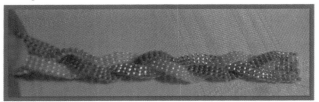

Braid the 3 legs.

Step 8.

Holding on to the open edges, measure your piece. Hold it up to your barrette finding. Add or remove rows to each of your legs to get the piece to the desired length, taking into account you will be adding 5 more rows after the braided section.

Step 9.

Straight stitch 5 rows of 9 beads each in random color order to the loose ends of the braid.

Step 10.

Glue the piece to the finding and allow to dry.

Step 11.

Reinforce the attachment to the finding by weaving the thread through the beads on the edges and up and down the back of the finding.

Charming

Windows

CHARMING WINDOWS BRACELET

A wonderful way to use up your "leftover" crystals, the

Charming Windows Bracelet can be done in any color combination and using any charms you like. Make it in autumn colors with leaf charms. Make it in pastel colors and use Easter egg charms. Make it in neutrals and hang pieces of picture jasper. Unleash your imagination!

SUPPLIES AND TOOLS

Each window of this bracelet measures ¾ of an inch if you only count one side (adjacent windows share a side). 8 windows and a slider clasp attached as shown results in a 6 5/8 inch bracelet.

4mm bicone crystals in various colors (93 for a 6 5/8 inch bracelet)

Size 11 seed beads in colors similar to the crystals

Size 15 seed beads in colors similar to the crystals

Size 15 metallic charlottes (optional)

6 to 9 small charms

Clasp

Size 12 needle

Fireline 6LB/SIZE D .008" avg.dia. Crystal

Step 1.

Pick up 8 size 11 seed beads. Leaving a 6 inch tail, tie a knot, forming a circle with the beads. Work the thread through 4 of the beads, so that the thread comes out opposite the knot.

Step 2.

Working in right angle weave, create 5 X 5 square box. The

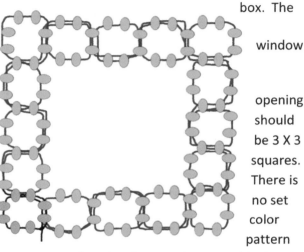

window opening should be 3 X 3 squares. There is no set color pattern to use. Use colors that fit your theme and look pretty together.

Step 3.

Work the thread through so that it comes out on an edge ready to add another 5 X 5 square. When threading through the top-middle square, string on about 5 size 15 seed beads (or metallic charlottes), and a charm. Work the thread through this little loop a couple of times.

Step 4.

Repeat step 3 until you have 6 or 7 windows with charms. Add one more empty window.

Step 5.

Lay on crystals. Go through each crystal twice with your thread. To help create a color blending effect, don't change color crystals exactly where you changed colors on the seed beads. So for example if you have 4 seed bead squares, 2 in color A and 2 in color B, lay on 3 crystals in color A and 1 in color B.

Step 6.

Create crisp edges by filling in the gaps between squares with size 15 seed beads. Use colors that are similar to the colors of the size 11 seed beads and crystals nearby.

Step 7.

Attach clasp. Cover thread with size 15 seed beads or metallic charlottes. Work thread through the loops a few times to secure. A 5-loop slider clasp works nicely for this bracelet

XOXO

Bracelet

XOXO Bracelet

Celebrate hugs and kisses with this bracelet that is just as much fun to make as it is to wear. The bracelet pictured measures 7 ¼ inches. Make the Xs and Os separately, join them and add a clasp.

SUPPLIES AND TOOLS

39 red 4mm bicone crystals

52 opal 4mm bicone crystals

Size 11 red seed beads

Size 11 white seed beads

Size 15 red seed beads

Size 15 white seed beads

Clasp

Size 12 needle

Fireline 6LB/SIZE D .008" avg.dia. Crystal

Step 1.

Leaving a 6 inch tail, pick up 9 size 11 red seed beads. Bring ends together and tie a knot. Thread needle through 5 seed beads, so that the thread

comes out opposite the knot. This will form the first trapezoid of one of the red Os. It takes 13 trapezoids to make an O.

Step 2.

Pick up 7 size 11 red seed beads. Thread needle through the top 2 beads of the first trapezoid, and the first 4 beads just picked up.

Step 3.

Working to keep the piece flat, continue using curved right angle weave to create 13 trapezoids. The side with 3 seed beads should always be on the outside.

Step 4.

Lay red crystals and red size 15 seed beads on top of each trapezoid. Thread the needle through the crystal and size 15 seed beads twice.

Step 5.

Smooth the edges by stringing red size 15 seed beads in the gaps between trapezoids. Fill in all gaps on the outer curve of the circle. On the inner curve, fill in some gaps, but leave others. The key here is to keep the piece flat. Too many beads in the inner curve will cause the piece to ripple. The gaps are not as large on the inner curve, so the inner curve needs less smoothing.

Step 6.

Repeat steps 1 through 5 two more times, so you have 3 red Os.

Step 7.

Start your first white X by picking up 8 size 11 white seed beads. Leaving a 6 inch tail, tie the ends together. Work thread through 4 beads, so needle comes out opposite the knot.

Step 8.

Pick up 6 size 11 white seed beads. Pass thread through the top 2 beads from the previous step, and the first 4 beads just picked up. Continue in white right angle weave until you have 7 squares in a line.

Step 9.

Work the thread back through 3 squares, and through 2 side beads on the middle square. This is to position the thread for making the cross of the X.

Step 10.

Pick up 6 white size 11 seed beads, and start forming the cross leg of the X.

Step 11.

Add 2 more squares in white size 11 seed beads.

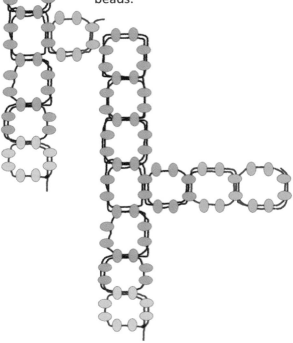

Step 12.

Work the thread back through 4 squares, so that it is poised to add squares to the other side.

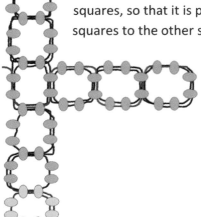

Step 13.

Add on 3 size 11 seed framework for more squares in white beads. This finishes the the X.

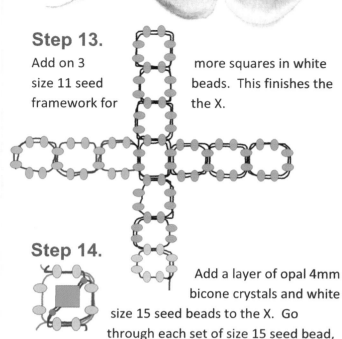

Step 14.

Add a layer of opal 4mm bicone crystals and white size 15 seed beads to the X. Go through each set of size 15 seed bead, crystal, and size 15 seed bead twice with your thread.

Step 15.

Smooth edges of the X by stringing white size 15 seed beads into the gaps between squares. the

Step 16.

Repeat steps 7 through 15 to make 3 more white Xs, so you have 4 white Xs in total.

Step 17.

Join the Xs and Os. Thread needle through the beads a few times for strength. Be careful not to force the needle through and break a bead.

Step 18.

Attach clasp. Use size 15 seed beads to cover the thread used to attach the clasp.